# THE WALRUS

By
**Carl R. Green**
**William R. Sanford**

Edited By
**Dr Howard Schroeder**

Macmillan

Copyright © 1988
by Macmillan Children's Books
A division of Macmillan Publishers Ltd
4 Little Essex Street
London WC2R 3LF and Basingstoke

Original copyright © 1986 by Crestwood House Inc.

Produced and designed by
Baker Street Productions
Mankato, Minnesota, USA

Illustration Credits:

Nadine Orabona/Stock Concepts: Cover 7, 10
James Allen: 5
Johnny Johnson/DRK Photo: 9, 17, 18, 25, 26, 30
Stephen J. Krasemann/DRK Photo: 13, 37, 44
Lynn M. Stone: 14, 41
John W. Matthews/DRK Photo: 20, 28, 33
Joe Branney/Tom Stack & Assoc: 29
Lynn Rogers: 42

British Library Cataloguing in Publication Data

Green, Carl R.
  The walrus. – (Animals in danger).
  1. Walruses – Juvenile literature
  I. Title II. Sanford, William R.
  III. Schroeder, Howard IV. Series
  599.74'7 QL737.P62

ISBN 0 333 47040 0

**Note to the reader**
In this book there are some words which are
printed in bold type. This shows that the word
is listed in the glossary. The glossary gives a
brief explanation of words which may be new
to you.

1438    £4.50     599
GREEN

GREEN + SANFORD
ANIMALS IN DANGER
THE WALRUS

1438            £4.50      599
GREEN

# TABLE OF CONTENTS

# INTRODUCTION:

'Hey! Peggy, look at this!' Manuel called. 'Have you ever seen a stranger looking animal?'

Peggy ran to the outdoor pool where Manuel was standing. All of the **oceanarium's** sea creatures were exciting, she thought. 'What could be funnier than the penguins?' Peggy asked.

Manuel pointed to seven fat, brown animals that were sleeping in the sun. At first, they looked like extra large seals. But Peggy noticed something.

'I know! See those long tusks? Those are walruses!' she shouted. 'And those whiskers! They look like my Uncle Jack.'

'I bet your Uncle Jack doesn't weigh well over 2000 kilograms,' a strange voice said.

Peggy and Manuel looked around. A young woman was smiling at them. She was wearing a special oceanarium jacket.

'My name is Mary Chung. I work here at the oceanarium,' the woman said. 'As you can see, we have everything from one-year-old walrus calves to full-grown adults. What would you like to know?'

'Tell us everything!' Manuel told their new friend.

'Well, these are Pacific walruses,' Mary said. 'The Atlantic walrus is a smaller animal. The walrus belongs to a family called the *Odobenidae*. That's a Latin name

4

*Look at those whiskers!*

that means "Animal that walks with its teeth". You see, the walrus sometimes uses its tusks like ice picks. It jabs them into the ice to pull itself out of the water.'

She held her hands well apart. 'Pacific walruses have tusks that average 61 centimetres long. They weigh between 1.4 and 1.8 kilograms each. A tusk is really an extra-long tooth'.

'Something's wrong,' Peggy said. 'I know that the little ones haven't grown their tusks yet. But why does that big walrus over there look as though it doesn't have any tusks?'

'A few of our walruses wear their tusks down by rubbing them on the concrete,' Mary replied. 'That also happens in nature. Many wild walruses have worn down, broken tusks.'

'Do they ever fight with their tusks?' Manuel asked.

'Yes, the males fight to show who's dominant,' Mary told him. 'The two fighters lift their heads and stab downward with their tusks. After a few slashes, the weaker walrus usually backs off.'

'I'm glad my teeth don't grow that long,' Peggy laughed.

Mary smiled. 'Well, if you were a walrus, you wouldn't say that,' she said. 'Tusks are quite useful. As well as using them as weapons, a resting walrus can use its tusks to hold its head up off the ice. Some experts think that the tusks are also useful when the walrus is digging up **clams** from the ocean floor.'

A voice called Mary's name over the loudspeaker. 'That's for me,' Mary told them. 'I have to babysit for a sick shark.'

Peggy and Manuel waved as Mary left. Manuel pulled on Peggy's arm. 'Come on! Let's go over to the shark tank,' he said.

Peggy didn't hear him. 'The sign says that walruses live in the Arctic,' she told him. 'How do they survive the cold winters there? And how do they eat a clam? Forget the sharks. I still have a thousand things to find out about the walrus!'

**Walruses sunning themselves at an oceanarium.**

# CHAPTER ONE:

Watch a walrus hump and thump its way across a rocky Arctic beach. It moves like a big caterpillar with flippers. Now watch that same animal dive into the sea. Like a fat submarine, the walrus glides smoothly through the cold water.

Many thousands of years ago, the **ancestors** of the walrus lived along the Pacific coast of the Americas. These early walruses looked something like the modern sea lion. **Experts** believe that these early walruses later spread into the Atlantic Ocean. The Atlantic herds survived, but the Pacific herds died out.

As the walrus moved northward in the Atlantic Ocean, it adapted to the cold water of the North Atlantic. Animals which look much like today's walruses developed in the cold Arctic waters thousands of years ago. Later, some of the herds migrated across the Arctic Sea and found rich feeding grounds in the Bering Sea. Over thousands of years, these herds spread out and found a home in the North Pacific waters. They grew larger in size than their Atlantic cousins. Today, they are known as the Pacific walrus.

*These walruses are on Round Island, Alaska, on the Bering Sea.*

# A creature of many names

Hundreds of years ago, Viking sailors saw some strange sea creatures sunning themselves on the ice. They called them *hvalross*, the 'whale horse'. The walrus doesn't look like either a whale or a horse, but the name stuck.

By whatever name, the walrus is an air-breathing **mammal** that lives in the ocean. As with the young of all mammals, walrus calves are born alive and are fed with the female's milk. Unlike the whales, however, the walrus spends part of its life on land. Experts put the walrus in the same family as the seals, the *pinnipedea*. The Pacific walrus's scientific name is *Odobenus rosmarus divergens*. The Atlantic walrus is *Odobenus rosmarus rosmarus*.

*Viking sailors gave the walrus its name.*

10

# A big body to cope with Arctic cold

Among seagoing mammals, only whales and elephant seals are larger than the walrus. The walrus's great size helps to keep in its body heat in a **habitat** where freezing cold is common. The largest wild walrus ever killed weighed 1557 kilograms. Experts think that the biggest males, which are known as bulls, may weigh two tonnes or more. A walrus bulging with **blubber** is sometimes bigger around than it is long!

The average walrus is somewhat smaller. Atlantic males average 680 kilograms and are three metres long. The smaller females, which are called cows, average 567 kilograms and are 2.7 metres long. The larger Pacific bulls weigh 907 kilograms and grow to over 3.4 metres long. Pacific cows weigh 635 kilograms and are three metres long.

The walrus's huge body is covered by a thick, brown skin. The skin varies in thickness from 1.3 centimetres to 3.8 centimetres. The tough skin protects the walrus from the cold and from the tusks of other walruses. Younger animals are also covered by coarse hair just over a centimetre long. Older bulls lose much of the hair on their heads and shoulders. As walruses grow older, their skins also become scarred and wrinkled. The bulls develop large bumps called tubercles on their necks and shoulders.

# Thick blubber and warm blood

The walrus's body is well adapted to withstand the cold. Like all mammals it is warm-blooded. It has a body temperature close to that of humans at 37° Centigrade. In the Arctic, the walrus must maintain its body heat in very cold weather when the temperature can drop to −29° C.

To stay alive in that frozen world, the walrus depends on a thick blanket of blubber, or body fat. Blubber varies in thickness from about 2.54 centimetres to almost 12.7 centimetres on the shoulders and chest. The flippers do not have any blubber, but they are kept warm with an extra supply of blood. Blubber also provides an energy supply when food is hard to find.

Even in the coldest winds, the walruses haul themselves out from the water to lie on the ice. They don't seem to notice the cold. In fact, if the temperature rises above 5° C, the walruses act as if they're too hot! They cool down by waving their back flippers to get rid of the extra body heat.

# Useful tusks and whiskers

A walrus starts growing extra-long **canine teeth,** called tusks, at about six months of age. For another year, the tusks remain hidden under the upper lip. The tusks continue growing well into the walrus's adult life. Bulls have longer tusks than the cows. The tusks average about 36 centimetres for Atlantic bulls, and 61 centimetres long for the Pacific type.

*Sleeping bulls show off their long tusks.*

*A walrus uses its whiskers to help it find food on the ocean floor.*

Up to 600 whiskers, called vibrissae, grow from pads in the upper lip of the walrus. These whiskers give the walrus its funny look. Many whiskers grow up to 12.7 centimetres in length, and some are as thick as a pencil. The whiskers signal 'food' to the walrus when they brush against clams and other **molluscs** in the mud of the seafloor.

# Well-adapted senses

The walrus's senses are well adapted to its Arctic habitat. Its eyes bulge from sockets located high on its head. When it wants to look at something, the walrus simply rolls its eyes without moving its head. The walrus's sight works best at close range. It's also better at spotting moving objects than those that don't move. As with other **pinnipeds,** the walrus's eyes work well in or out of the water.

The walrus depends on its sense of smell to warn of danger. A walrus which hears a strange sound will raise its head and sniff the air with wide-open nostrils. Then it will blow out a puff of air with a loud snort as a warning to its herd. A walrus can locate other walruses by smell long before they can be seen. Experts say that this shouldn't be very hard, for walruses have a strong body odour!

Small openings on each side of the head carry sound to the walrus's inner ear. Eskimos say that a walrus can hear their hunting calls from 1.5 kilometres or more away. The walrus does not rely on hearing to warn of danger, however. Experts believe that the walrus uses its hearing mostly to listen to the calls of other walruses.

# Slow on land, quicker in the water

A walrus has two pairs of flippers for swimming and moving about on land. The front flippers average about 61 centimetres in length and about 38 centimetres across. The back pair are 15 centimetres shorter. Each flipper has five small claws that help the walrus cling to slippery rocks and ice.

When it hauls itself out on to land, the walrus humps along like a giant caterpillar. To move its huge body around, it lifts its back end up and swings forward on its front flippers. For all this awkward movement, walruses sometimes travel long distances on land. Herds have been spotted which have gone 24 kilometres over rocks and hills to find open water.

In the water, the walrus uses its back flippers to paddle along at about six kilometres per hour. That same walrus can swim at 32 kilometres per hour when chased by a boat, however. When diving for food, the walrus can stay under water for up to ten minutes. During a deep dive, the heartbeat slows from its normal 150 beats a minute to only fifteen beats a minute.

Another aid to swimming are the **'pharyngeal** pouches'. These are balloon-like sacs located below the walrus's throat. When filled with air, these pouches act

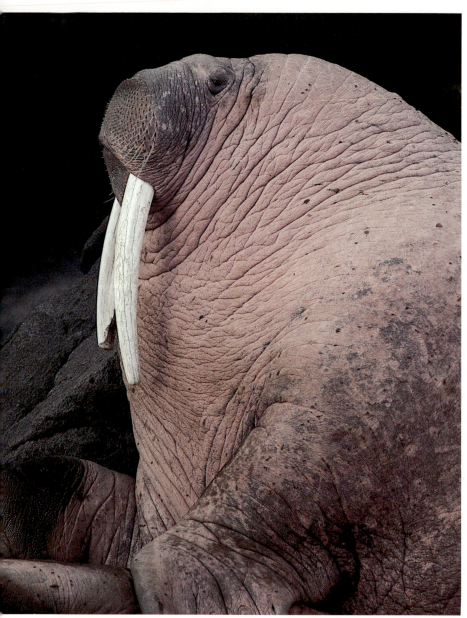

*Balloon-like sacs are located below the walrus's throat. The sacs can be filled with air to help the walrus float.*

17

like water wings to hold the walrus's head out of the water. The bulls also use the pouches to make their mating calls.

# A long-lived animal

Walruses can live as long as forty years. They mature by the age of four or five. Thus, a cow has many years in which to mate and give birth to calves. The bulls do not mate until they are ten to fifteen, however. Only a large, strong bull can win a cow as a mate.

The bull's search for a mate takes place in a remote Arctic habitat. Let's take a closer look at how the walrus has adapted to life in the Arctic cold.

*Walrus bulls will sometimes fight for mating rights.*

# CHAPTER TWO:

The Far North is the only place you can see a walrus in the wild. The Pacific herds range from the Bering Sea to the northern waters of the Chukchi Sea. The nearest land areas are Alaska and Siberia. The Atlantic herds can be found near northern Canada, Greenland and in the Laptev Sea off the USSR. Except when it **migrates**, the walrus never goes far from land. It prefers shallow water between 15 and 18 metres deep.

# A yearly migration

Atlantic walruses don't migrate very far. When summer comes, however, the Pacific walruses migrate northward to feeding grounds in the Chukchi Sea. Some of these animals will travel as far as 3200 kilometres. Along the way, the walruses rest on floating ice islands called ice floes. As long as the floe is moving in the right direction, they seem happy to accept a free ride. If the **current** changes, a walrus will swim on until it finds another ride going north.

The summer days are very long in the Land of the Midnight Sun. On 21 June, the longest day of the year, the sun never sets at all. But the summer lasts for only two months. In September, new ice starts to form in open water. Most of the walruses turn southward, but they don't seem to be in any hurry. If they find a good bed of clams, they may stay in that spot for several weeks. At other times, they swim for many miles across open sea before they find a resting place. Some of the

*A walrus will often rest on an ice floe.*

20

tough old males do not migrate. These bulls wait out the winter in the $-2.7°$ C of the Arctic waters.

The winter migration takes the Pacific herds back to southern Alaskan waters. In a similar way, Atlantic walruses turn southward to Hudson Bay or the waters near Greenland. Protected by blubber built up during the summer, the walruses can face long months of snow and freezing winds. The pale winter sun comes up for only a few hours each day.

# An ice-loving animal

Experts call the walrus a 'pagophilic' animal, or one that loves ice! The herds never go too far from the edge of the ice pack. Given a choice between land or ice, the walrus almost always chooses the ice. Hundreds of walruses sometimes try to haul themselves out on to a single ice floe. If the floe is unstable, it may tip up and dump all of the walruses into the sea!

Experts think that the ice gives the walrus a perfect habitat. Few **predators** live there, for one thing. For another, the cold keeps down the **parasites** and disease germs which often attack other animals that live close to each other. Lastly, the ice gives the walrus a floating 'island' from which to dive for food.

The ice-loving walrus is also a very social animal. Except for a few old males, they are usually seen in herds that can number from ten to a thousand or more. The herd often gathers on a small island that the Eskimos call an *oogli*. An *oogli* is only a resting place, however. The walrus must dive to the sea bottom for its food.

# A seafood diet

One expert counted over 65 different marine creatures eaten by the walrus. The walrus's favourite foods, however, are molluscs such as clams and mussels. A walrus also eats sandworms, whelks, sea urchins, starfish, hermit crabs and sea snails. It sometimes feeds

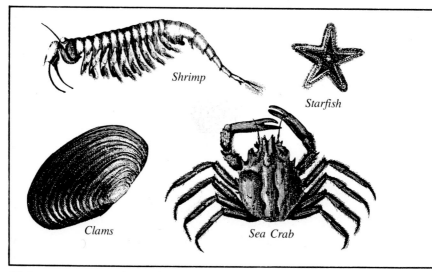

**Walruses eat a variety of seafood.**

on **algae** and the roots of sea grasses. Although it is not usually a hunter, some walruses will eat the flesh of dead whales and seals.

To get to a clam dinner, a walrus dives almost straight down into the water. At the bottom, the walrus roots in the soft mud with its muzzle. Its sensitive whiskers tell the animal where the clams are buried. At one time, experts thought the walrus used its tusks to dig up the bottom. But then they noticed that tuskless walruses were just as fat as the others. Perhaps the tusks only help plough up the mud as the walrus turns its head back and forth.

The walrus has to work hard and fast. It must find and eat over 45 kilograms of food a day. Instead of crushing the shells, the walrus sucks out the meat from

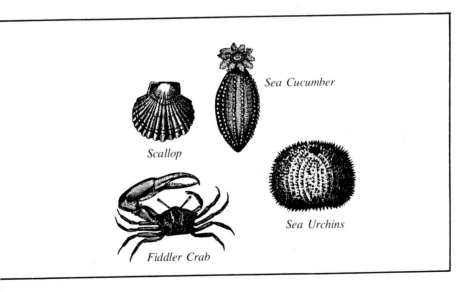

*Sea Cucumber*

*Scallop*

*Sea Urchins*

*Fiddler Crab*

clams, whelks and other molluscs. Since the creatures it eats are small, a walrus must find thousands of molluscs to make a meal.

After the herd cleans out the food supply in one place, it moves on to another feeding spot. Experts believe that this feeding pattern helps keep the sea floor well supplied with life. The walruses dig up the ocean bottom and scatter half-eaten molluscs. This messy process provides **nutrients** to support the tiny creatures at the bottom of the food chain. With plenty of **plankton** to feed on, a new crop of molluscs will grow in time for the herd's next visit.

# An animal with few enemies

The walrus has few enemies other than humans. Only the killer whale and the polar bear prey on the walrus. Killer whales have been known to pick off a calf from a group of swimming walruses. The herd may panic at the sight of the sharp-toothed killers. If that happens, a small walrus may be crushed in the rush to get out of the water. If it decides to fight, however, a full-grown bull is a good match for a killer whale.

More often, the attack comes from a polar bear. Three metres in length, these predators usually attack cows and their calves. The walrus's best protection is

*A walrus surfaces from its best protection, the water.*

to get into the water. If trapped, however, it fights back with its tusks. Faced with those wicked weapons, the bear often backs away.

Most attacks by polar bears come during the summer. That's when the walrus herds migrate north to polar bear territory. Let's pick up a Pacific walrus herd in the spring as it begins its yearly life cycle.

# CHAPTER THREE:

The Far North is a world of harsh, cold beauty. Only a handful of hardy mammals can live there. Of these, the walrus and other pinnipeds have adapted to a life cycle split between the land and the sea.

*A walrus's life is split between the land and sea.*

26

# Calves arrive in the spring

The long Arctic winter is over. Under the warm sun, ice floes break loose from the edge of the ice pack and drift away. Small groups of walruses rest on these floating ice islands. They are heading north to their summer feeding grounds.

A calf is born during the night. The newborn walrus is just over a metre long and weighs about 59 kilograms. The mother walrus holds the calf under her flippers and warms it with her own body heat. She is a good mother, but she lets the calf know what must be done. When the calf refuses to dive into the cold water, the cow pushes it in. The newborn calf can swim, but on longer trips it rides on the cow's back. At night, the cow and her calf sleep apart from the rest of the herd. Calves are sometimes killed when an adult walrus rolls over on them!

The calf lives on the cow's rich milk for the first six months of its life. After that, it begins eating scraps of food left by the other walruses. At one year, the calves will have tripled their birth weight. Tiny tusks, only 2.5 centimetres long, stick out from their upper lips. By the time the calves are two years old, many cows will have given birth to another calf. When they're four, the males leave to join an all-male herd. The females stay in the same herd as their mothers.

*In the spring the herds move northward.*

The herds move northward as the ice melts. They stop often to feed in shallow waters. A year-old calf wanders off from its cow and barks in a high, scared voice. Quickly, the cow swims to her calf and pushes it back to the ice floe. Other walruses watch to see that the calf is safe. An adult walrus will come to the aid of any calf that is in trouble.

# Summer brings long, sunny days

The brief summer arrives in July and August. By now, the herd has travelled over 1600 kilometres. The walruses haven't been in a hurry. They swim for a

28

while, then haul out on a rocky *oogli*. It's a good time for sunning.

One big bull has been feeding in deep, cold water. When he hauls out, his skin is a pale bluish-white. It looks as though he's been drained of blood! While he was diving, much of his blood supply stayed deep inside his body so that it stayed warm. After a few minutes on the surface, the blood returns to the skin area. The bull is soon his usual rosy-brown colour.

*A long time in cold water caused this bull to be almost white in colour.*

*Walruses like to soak up the sun!*

The walruses lie in the sun most of the day. Seabirds land on the walruses to pick at the sea lice and other insects that live on their skin. The younger walruses are shedding their old hair, ready to grow a new coat. The all-bull herds often go without food for days at a time. The mixed herds, however, have cows who must feed their calves. The nursing cows and the younger walruses dive for food every day.

The sleeping bulls hate to be bothered. When one bull rolls over on to a sleeping neighbour, a fight breaks out. The sleeper wakes up and slaps the other walrus with its flippers. The second bull slaps back. They both bellow loudly. Other bulls wake up and add to the noise. The fighters raise their tusks and slash at each other. The smaller walrus soon gives up. He backs down, blood flowing from a cut on his head. Quiet returns to the herd.

# The herds turn southward in the autumn

The short Arctic summer soon fades into autumn. By September, all but some of the older bulls are moving south. New ice is forming around the ice floes. The ice sometimes keeps the walruses from hauling themselves out of the water when they want to.

The walruses don't seem to notice the freezing cold. The deep layers of blubber built up during the summer keep them warm. The walrus's thick skull comes in handy when ice forms over the clam beds. The animals open breathing holes by butting at the ice with their heads. The ice here is 7.5 centimetres thick, but the walruses break through with ease.

A lone walrus is swimming far behind the migrating herd. It is a **rogue** bull, a walrus that prefers meat to molluscs. The rogue slips up to a sleeping seal and uses its front flippers to crush the smaller pinniped against its body. Then it rips the seal's skin with its tusks and sucks out the meat and blubber. A rogue is easy to spot, for its tusks are stained yellow-brown by seal oil. It probably learned to like meat by feeding on dead seals when it was a calf.

The days are growing shorter and the ice is pressing southward, driving the walruses back into the Bering Sea. At night, the walruses hook their tusks into the edge of an ice floe and sleep in the water.

# Winter days are short and cold

By mid-winter, the pale sun rises for only a few hours a day. The walruses spend most of their time in the water. But even on the coldest days they brave the cold to rest on an icy shore.

Huge bulls appear in the water near the ice floe. They swim back and forth, trying to attract the cows. The bulls make sounds like a chiming clock. Along with this bell-like sound, they click their teeth, whistle and roar. A young cow joins one of the bulls in the water. The pair flip over in the water, and rise to the surface to breath through holes in the ice. Finally, they turn stomach-to-stomach to mate, their flippers pressing their huge bodies together. Fifteen months from now, a new calf will be born. The bull will not be there, though. After the mating is over, he returns to an all-male herd.

The ice itself can be a danger. Snow often covers cracks in the floes. A calf falls into one of these hidden cracks and can't get out. The cow hears its cries and hurries to the rescue. She chops at the ice with her tusks. The tusks work like twin pickaxes. Chips of ice fly as she works. After twenty minutes of chopping, the calf is able to escape from the crack.

The walruses do not all migrate together. Herds of bulls and cows without calves travel faster. These groups reach the winter feeding grounds a month ahead of the slower-moving cows and calves. The walruses don't keep to a timetable. If a herd finds a rich feeding ground, it will stay for several weeks. Only when the ice closes off their breathing holes do they move on.

One group of fifteen walruses stops to feed in a small bay. A sudden shift in the ice traps them, but they are safe as long as there is food. When the last mollusc is eaten, they have to cross 16 kilometres of rough ice to reach the open sea. Weak from hunger, they cannot withstand the bitter cold. Only two cows make it to safety with their calves. The others die on the ice, their flippers frozen.

Left alone, about three per cent of the herd dies each year. Accidents, fights, disease and attacks by predators kill off the weaker animals. Despite these dangers, the herds grow rapidly if they are left alone. Thousands of years ago, however, something happened to break their peaceful life cycle. Humans arrived and began hunting the walrus.

*A walrus hunting party rests on an ice floe.*

# CHAPTER FOUR:

Long before history was written down, people hunted the walrus in its Arctic habitat. Walrus bones have been found in the ruins of towns and villages that are thousands of years old. A hunter who killed one of these huge mammals would surely have been a hero to the entire village.

The Eskimos who lived in the Far North were walrus hunters. They made warm coats, rope and canoes from the tough hide. The oil burned clean and warm in their lamps, and the meat fed people and sledge dogs alike. The Eskimos even made drumheads from the stomachs.

# Large-scale hunting begins

Hunting by Eskimos and other natives did not greatly reduce the number of walruses. In the early 1600s, however, people from Europe joined in the hunt. The hunters sailed north to the shallow offshore waters where the walruses fed on molluscs. In 1604, an English sailor saw 600 walrus killed in less than six hours. Other sailors reported large kills in the waters north of Norway and Russia.

Eskimos killed one walrus at a time, but European hunters wiped out entire herds. The hunters came in from the sea and used lances to kill the sleeping animals. The dead and dying walruses were piled up along the beach. Trapped behind the wall of bodies, many of the survivors could not reach the water. That gave the hunters time to kill more.

The hunters thought that there would always be plenty of walruses. But the herds slowly became smaller. In 1824, for example, Norwegian hunters took almost 700 walrus hides from Bear Island. Forty years later, the hunters found only one walrus on that same island. By the 1930s, the Norwegians were forced to go deep into Arctic waters to kill walruses.

# Hunting too many walruses

The early settlers in North America found Atlantic walruses as far south as Nova Scotia. Hunters killed thousands of them off the coasts of Canada and Greenland. Between 1905 and 1909, for example, hunters from Scotland took 3000 hides. In addition, thousands of wounded animals escaped, only to die at sea. The Scots said that the herds seemed to be getting smaller every year.

Walrus tusks were in great demand. Russian traders joined in the hunt in the late 1800s. They killed thousands of walruses in the Bering Sea. By the early 1900s, the walrus herds of the Pribilof Islands were almost gone. Naturalists believe that the total number of walruses fell as low as 50 000. Most of the survivors lived in remote places where hunters couldn't reach them easily.

The United States protected the walrus under the Marine Mammal Protection Act of 1972. This law did not end the hunting of all walruses, however. The law allows the Alaskan Eskimos to kill about 3000 walruses each year. The Eskimos are given this quota because walrus-hunting is part of their culture.

After the large-scale killing stopped, the walrus herds began to grow again. Today, the Atlantic walrus numbers about 30 000. The Pacific herds are larger. The Bering and Chukchi now seas support over 200 000 walruses.

# Walrus tusks are in demand

In the past, Eskimos hunted the walrus with canoes and harpoons. Now, they use motorboats and rifles. Some Eskimos freeze the meat to eat during the winter. But more and more, the hunters take only the ivory tusks. Living costs are high in the North, and the hard creamy-white ivory tusks that are taken are a big source of income.

A 'raw' tusk is worth only a few hundred pounds. But tourists will pay high prices for carved ivory. Eskimo carvers make rings, statues, letter openers and other small items from the tusks. A good ivory carver can make hundreds of pounds a day. This 'easy' income has created a demand for more ivory, but the demand can be filled only by killing more walruses.

Alaska and Canada have taken steps to control the selling of tusks. Canada forbids the sale of uncarved ivory, for example. Alaska tries to control the problem by making the ivory carvers take out a licence. Some of the Eskimos are also trying to solve the problem. They put limits on the number of walruses the hunters can kill in a day. They know that too much killing may drive the animals away. If that happens, no one will have any ivory.

*These carvings were made by Eskimos from walrus ivory.*

# New dangers to the habitat

The walrus's habitat is still in danger. Huge oil deposits have been found under the Bering Sea. The world needs oil, and plans are being made to drill for this new supply. But taking out the oil means more people, more ships and more damage to the habitat. No one knows just what this will do to the walrus.

The walrus also faces the loss of some of its feeding grounds. Companies are planning to bring in huge **dredgers** to harvest the rich clam beds. The dredgers are so good at their job, however, that they may destroy the clam beds. If that happens, the walruses may not be able to find the vast amounts of food they need. Even if the dredgers stay away, there may already be too many walruses for the food supply that now exists.

Despite these problems, experts hope the walrus will survive. They know that these highly-adaptable animals have done nearly as well in captivity as they have in the wild.

# CHAPTER FIVE:

To see most sea creatures in their natural habitat is not easy. But you can see sharks, whales, seals and other wild animals at special marine 'zoos' called oceanariums.

Some animals are harder to keep at an oceanarium than others. It used to be that every time someone tried to keep walruses, for example, the animals died. Moving these huge animals was only the first part of the problem. The second was to help these ice-loving animals adjust to a warm climate.

# First, you catch four calves

Experts at Marineland of the Pacific, in California, thought they knew how to solve the problem. First, they built a large saltwater tank at the oceanarium near Los Angeles. Then they sent a team to Alaska to capture four calves. The experts thought that young walruses would be more likely to adjust to their new home.

In the spring of 1961, three collectors went to Alaska's St Lawrence Island. On the second day, they found a cow and a young calf floating on a large ice floe. Their Eskimo guide shot the cow and the collectors picked up the frightened calf. If the guide hadn't killed the cow, she would never have let the people take her calf.

Later that day, the collectors took a second female calf. After one more week of hunting, they added two male calves. All of the calves were about six weeks old and weighed about 57 kilograms. The young walruses weren't afraid of people. They even rolled over so people could rub their stomachs.

The calves huddled next to each other to keep warm. But mostly they snorted and barked to show that they were hungry. The island didn't have any milk, so the walruses were fed a mixture of peanut oil, ground-up clams, and vitamins. The calves were also given shots to keep them from getting ill. When the young walruses were ready to travel, they were caged and put on an aeroplane. Three days later they landed in Los Angeles.

# Adjusting to a new life

The Marineland experts put the calves in their new tank. They put blocks of ice in the water, but the warm sun melted it. Could the walruses adjust to water so much warmer than the Bering Sea? The walruses didn't seem to mind. They quickly made themselves at home in the filtered sea water.

Four times a day, the keepers gave the calves a mix of ground-up fish and clams, whipping cream and vitamins. The walruses drank from giant 'baby bottles'. By the time they were six months old, the calves were drinking 53 litres of this mixture a day. The fast-growing calves gained 500 grams a day on the rich diet.

The Marineland people gave names to the calves. The two females were called Priscilla and Petula. The males were named Woofy and Farouk. Each walrus learned to answer when the keepers called it by name.

*The calves grew quickly at Marineland.*

# Life wasn't all fun and games

The young walruses got along well. They played chase and nipped at each other's flippers. Sometimes they rubbed noses in a sloppy walrus 'kiss'. After swimming, they hauled themselves out of the water to sleep in the sun. When they cut new teeth, they sucked on their flippers to help reduce the pain.

The keepers decided not to teach any tricks to the walruses. Seals learn tricks quickly, and walruses might be able to do the same. Visitors enjoyed the walruses

*Visitors at Marineland don't expect the walruses to do tricks.*

just as they were, however. In addition, the training process might have put a strain on the walruses. This could make them catch diseases more easily.

As it was, the keepers had to work very hard to keep the walruses healthy. One problem involved skin lice. The keepers had to pick the lice off by hand because insect sprays would have made the walruses ill. One by one, the walruses also picked up eye infections, skin rashes and breathing problems. Each time, the keepers nursed the calves back to health.

The concrete tanks created one more problem. Farouk, Priscilla and Petula rubbed their tusks against the concrete. They soon wore them down to short stumps. The constant rubbing caused gum infections. If animal doctors hadn't found the right medicine, the walruses would have died. The walruses also swallowed things that visitors dropped into their tanks. Sweet papers, for example, caused some of the walruses stomachaches.

# Marineland scores a first

By the time they were thirty months old, the calves were eating an adult diet of fish and clams. They grew fat on the rich food. The two males soon weighed over two tonnes each.

*The males soon weighed almost 2000 kilograms!*

As they matured, Woofy and Farouk started fighting over the females. The keepers had to put Woofy and Petula in one tank and Farouk and Priscilla in another. Several years later, Priscilla fell ill of a stomach disease. The doctors couldn't save her. When Woofy also died, Petula was put in Farouk's tank. Two new walruses were flown in from the Moscow Zoo. The new walruses were named Woolfy and Priscilla in honour of the first pair.

In 1975, Petula gave birth to the first walrus calf ever born in captivity. That calf died eighteen months later, but Petouk was born in 1978. The new Priscilla gave birth to Andrea that same year. The breeding programme was finally a success. Petula died in 1985, however, while trying to give birth to twins. Sadly, the rare twin calves could not be saved.

In 1982, Marineland added two new calves. These 'orphans' had been left on the Arctic ice when their mothers were killed. This filled the walrus tanks almost to overflowing. But no one minds having too many walruses. Each day, thousands of people stop at the walrus tanks. They all seem to enjoy looking at these huge seagoing mammals from the Far North.

# MAP:

*Walruses are found mostly in the shaded areas above.*

46

# GLOSSARY:

**algae:** *very tiny green plants that grow in water*

**ancestors:** *a relative who lived and died a long time ago*

**blubber:** *a very thick layer of fat found in warm-blooded sea animals. The blubber helps the animals to keep their body temperature at the right level*

**canine teeth:** *sharp pointed teeth used for tearing and ripping meat*

**clam:** *a shellfish with a double shell which clamps tightly together*

**current:** *a flow of water, air or electricity in a particular direction*

**dredger:** *a boat which carries machines for scraping up mud and other objects from the bottom of lakes, rivers or the sea*

**expert:** *someone who has studied a particular thing and knows a lot about it*

**habitat:** *the place where an animal makes its home*

**mammal:** *an animal which gives birth to live young which feed on their mother's milk*

**migrate:** *to move from one area to another to find fresh food or a different climate*

**mollusc:** *a type of sea animal with a soft body usually protected by a hard shell*

**nutrient:** *any substance that an animal or plant needs in order to grow*

**oceanarium:** *a kind of zoo for sea creatures and plants*

**parasite:** *any animal or plant which lives on or in another, usually causing harm*

**pharyngeal:** *describes the tube and cavity of the mouth and nose which connects to the windpipe*

**pinniped:** *a type of warm-blooded animal whose limbs have adapted to life in the water*

**plankton:** *very tiny sea animals that are food for the smallest fish*

**predator:** *an animal which hunts other animals*

**rogue:** *an animal which has turned savage. They live alone and will often kill*

# INDEX: